WITHDRAWN FROM COLLECTION VLE

D0852443

The beauty of this noble stream at almost any point, but especially in the commencement of this journey, when it winds it way among the Thousand Islands, can hardly be imagined. The number and constant successions of these islands, all green and richly wooded; their fluctuating size, their infinite variety of shapes; and the numberless combinations of beautiful forms which trees growing on them present: all forms a picture fraught with uncommon interest and pleasure.

— Charles Dickens, *American Notes for General Circulation*

To all my friends in the Thousand Islands:
Thank you for your support!

We have forged a connection beyond business
and you have found a place in my heart.

—George

"Summertime, and the livin' is easy."

– George Gerschwin

Historic wooden boats are a popular means of transportation in the Thousand Islands. Well-maintained and in pristine condition, many also grace classic boat shows.

PREVIOUS: The 1000 Islands Tower on Hill Island offers a spectacular view of the Thousand Islands Bridge as well as Georgina, Ash, and Wallace islands. **Lansdowne, ON**

FACING: Boldt Castle showing the Dove-Cote and the Power House. **Alexandria Bay, NY**

Copyright © 2016 George Fischer.

All rights reserved. No part of this book may be reproduced, stored in a retrieval system, or transmitted in any form or by any means without prior written permission from the photographer, George Fischer.

Design and captions by Catharine Barker National Graphics, Toronto, ON Canada

Copy Editor: E. Lisa Moses

Nimbus Publishing Limited
3731 Mackintosh Street
Halifax, NS Canada
B3K 5MB

Tel.: 902 455-4286

Printed in China

Library and Archives Canada Cataloguing in Publication

Fischer, George, 1954-, author

The Thousand Islands / George Fischer.

ISBN 978-0-9936941-2-7 (bound)

1. Thousand Islands (N.Y. and Ont.) —Pictorial works.   I. Title.

FC3095.T43F582 2014   971.3'7050222
C2014-901392-2

The Thousand Islands

GEORGE FISCHER

Boldt Castle floats on purple mist, as seen from Scenic View Park.
Alexandria Bay, NY

Morning mists rise from shimmering waters, punctuated by private islands housing castles and cottages. Midday sun and evening shadows greet cruise ships and yachts, canoes and kayaks. Waterfront towns offer music, theatre, and fine dining along with historic inns and B&Bs, expansive campgrounds, and welcoming hotels. This is the Thousand Islands Region, originally christened the "Garden of the Great Spirit" by the area's First Nations.

The St. Lawrence River has for centuries been the region's economic artery, pulsing with trade, commerce and recreation. In summertime, it becomes an immense playground that actually comprises more than 1800 islands and meanders for 50 miles (80 kilometers) between Canada and the United States. In addition to offering some of the world's best sightseeing and water sports, the region is a feast for the photographic eye – and I am pleased to share my views on this superb destination.

Historical highlights

The Thousand Islands Region has connected Canada and the U.S. since before they were nations. During the Gilded Age, it became a hugely popular vacation retreat for the rich and famous who purchased private islands, turning them into showpieces of distinctive architecture and wealth. Dozens of industrialists, merchants, and other business leaders such as George Pullman, creator of the railroad sleeping car; George Boldt of the Waldorf Astoria Hotel; Nathan Straus of Macy's; and Helena Rubenstein, queen of a global cosmetics

empire, built massive summer homes. Their presence attracted the media spotlight, garnered international fame, and led to a tourism boom.

The St. Lawrence River, which links the Great Lakes and the Atlantic Ocean, has long been an essential travel route in both peace and war. It has ferried tourists in luxury steamships, bootleggers during Prohibition, and soldiers during the War of 1812. The remains of those days are now major attractions for history buffs who can drop in on various venues, among them battle sites and military fortifications such as Kingston, Ontario's Fort Henry.

In 1959, the St. Lawrence Seaway became a modern passage for international trade, accommodating enormous commercial ships from around the world. Today, it also serves as a shortcut for more than 2000 pleasure craft annually.

The maritime life

With easily navigable waters and friendly ports of call, the Thousand Islands Region was a pleasure to photograph. During the May to October season, countless leisure craft – from luxury yachts to wooden runabouts – cruised through my photo frames with skippers and captains, crews and passengers waving happily for the lens. Also sailing past were comfortable tour boats taking thousands of visitors on journeys that can include everything from entertaining dinner cruises to an exploration of the islands with stops at the fabled Boldt and Singer castles. There, the well-preserved stone, elaborate cut-glass windows, and ornate furnishings

The Ivy Lea Club marina has watched five generations grow and play on the banks of the St. Lawrence River. **Lansdowne, ON**

exude the glamour, romance, and tragedy of previous lives. And in winter, as I shoot from a helicopter, the sites take on a surreal aura.

Also part of the area's legendary past was avid angler and U.S. president Ulysses S. Grant, whose discovery of recreational fishing there in the 1860s launched the exceptionally popular pursuit for both novices and seasoned anglers. The area is known for trophy-sized catches of salmon, trout, walleye, and bass as well as northern pike and muskellunge. Today, fishing trips guided by experts are a guaranteed way to snag those prizes.

Spectators and participants will enjoy Brockville Ontario's Tall Ships Festival and the 1000 Islands Hydroplane Regatta, as well as Kingston's Freshwater Sailing Festival, which attracts hundreds of competitive sailors and spectators from around the world. Those interested in maritime history will appreciate the Antique Boat Museum in Clayton, New York and the Marine Museum of the Great Lakes in Kingston, where visitors can browse through seven galleries exploring different aspects of shipping.

Cultural immersion

The Region's unique culture provides an endless supply of entertainment, education, and activities, with an impressive lineup of festivals and events offering many reasons to return time and again.

The scenic Thousand Islands Parkway stretches 25 mi. (40 km) along the St. Lawrence River.   **Landon Bay, Gananoque, ON**

The 1000 Islands Poker Run is one of the largest such events internationally with more than 50,000 spectators. Other top draws are the Kingston Sheep Dog Trials, Limestone City Blues Festival, and the Kingston Dragon Boat Festival.

The waterfront Thousand Islands Playhouse showcases Canadian talent, while the Gananoque Sculpture Park offers Canada's largest contemporary art exhibit. Gananoque, Ontario also boasts the Arthur Child Heritage Centre, Thousand Islands Boat Museum, and numerous antique stores. Visitors can also try their luck at the 18-hole championship Smuggler's Glen Golf Course or the Shorelines Casino Thousand Islands.

In Kingston, dubbed "The Limestone City," trolley tours escort guests through heritage and architectural rarities including Queen's University, the Penitentiary Museum, Bellevue House, City Hall, and the Royal Military College. In summertime, visitors can stop at the 215-year-old open-air Kingston Public Market for fresh produce, flowers, and other local delicacies.

Today, the Thousand Islands Region continues to grow in popularity, beckoning international guests with its varied shorelines, well-preserved history, and colorful culture. Small wonder, since it is still the Garden of the Great Spirit.

– George Fischer

The eastern edge of Heart Island supports Boldt
Castle's Power House and Clock Tower that once
housed a steam generator for electricity to the
island. Today, installations of images and displays
depict the region's turn-of-the-century lifestyle.
Alexandria Bay, NY

The *Pride of Baltimore* in full sail along the
St. Lawrence Seaway during its goodwill
summer cruise through the Great Lakes.
Near Brockville, ON

The Admiralty Islands create
channels for adventurous
paddlers to explore.
Near Gananoque, ON

Castle Rest on Calumet Island enjoyed its glory days in the late 1800s. It once comprised 30 rooms, several outbuildings, a lagoon, and a boathouse. After a fire decimated the structures in 1956, only a few of the surrounding buildings survived. The landmark water tower is the most recognizable.

Clayton, NY

Hub Island — also known as "Just Room Enough Island" —
meets the criteria as one of the Thousand Islands. To qualify for
island status, a land mass must be above water level all year,
and support at least one living tree.

Alexandria Bay, NY

Rock Island Lighthouse, commissioned in
1847, was one of six guiding lights along the
St. Lawrence River. The light was shut down
in 1955 and the island is now a state park.

Fishers Landing, NY

PREVIOUS: Dock lights glow in the morning mist as Heart Island and Boldt Castle emerge. Construction on the castle, commissioned by millionaire hotel magnate George Boldt as a tribute to his wife, began in 1900. The site was abandoned in 1904 when she passed away.
Alexandria Bay, NY

A sign in the Admirals Inn Restaurant and Lounge exudes neon energy.
Alexandria Bay, NY

The Thousand Islands Bridge system is a series of
five bridges connecting northern New York in the
United States with southeastern Ontario in Canada.

Near Lansdowne, ON

On a bright, crisp winter's day, skating at
Kingston City Hall's outdoor ice rink is a
favorite pastime.

Kingston, ON

PREVIOUS: Boldt Castle on Heart Island surveys
a lake vessel (laker) in the shipping channel
while Harbor Island (left) and Sunken Rock
Lighthouse (right) keep watch.

Alexandria Bay, NY

Gargoyles pop up in unexpected
places around Boldt Castle.

Alexandria Bay, NY

Multicolored umbrellas shade diners from the hot sun
as they survey the sailboats at Navy Point Marine.
Sackets Harbor, NY

NEXT: The Thousand Islands Bridge is illuminated
at dusk over the American Narrows section of the
Seaway. The longest American span is 800 ft. (240 m)
while the longest Canadian one is 750 ft. (230 m).
Near Alexandria Bay, NY

You're never too young to ride the Muskoka
chairs and chill out on Joel Stone Beach.
Gananoque, ON

A soft sunset forms warm, twisting furrows in the water off Riverside Drive.

Clayton, NY

St. Lawrence River Skiffs were used during the late 1800s by guides for rowing clients out to fishing spots. Ideal for stability and changing river conditions, the flat-bottomed boats are ideal to pull onto a beach for a picnic.

Ivy Lea, Lansdowne, ON

The nautical legacy of the
St. Lawrence River is preserved
by many who lovingly restore and
showcase the features of their
historical vessels.

Near Clayton, NY

Spicer Bay, known for its
great fishing, assumes an
abstract rippling pattern
as night closes in.

Clayton, NY

Boldt Castle stays frozen in time from October
until May when it again becomes accessible to
visitors by water. It is an official U.S. port of entry.

Alexandria Bay, NY

PREVIOUS: From Hill Island to Constance Island,
Georgina Island and the Canadian mainland, the
Canadian span of the Thousand Islands Bridge
system is 3330 ft. (1015 m).

Built in 1854, the Tibbetts Point Lighthouse is on
the National Register of Historic Places. Its Fresnel
lens is one of only 70 still in use in the U.S.

Cape Vincent (town), NY

PREVIOUS: The Rock Island Lighthouse lantern room now offers visitors a full bird's-eye view of the surroundings. The buildings and the island reopened to the public in 2013.

Fishers Landing, NY

Jaw-dropping speed churns up the water at the 1000 Islands Regatta & Festival for the nation's premier hydroplane boat race.

Brockville, ON

In spectacular fashion, a vintage Gar Wood runabout slices at high speed through the wake of a passing tour boat.

PREVIOUS: As the sun rises, it burns off the early morning river mist near the Brockville narrows.
Brockville, ON

Boldt Castle's Power House and Clock Tower resembles a medieval tower rising from the depths. It is connected to Heart Island by a stone footbridge.
Alexandria Bay, NY

The cottage on Zavikon Island enjoys a great deal of attention all summer long. Tour guides sometimes point out (erroneously) that the bridge connecting the two islands is the world's shortest international bridge. In fact, both the dwelling and its backyard are Canadian, with the international border off the southern shore.

Near Rockport, ON

Grass Point State Park juts into the American channel and captures an
impressive view of the American Span of the Thousand Islands Bridge.

Alexandria Bay, NY

PREVIOUS: Nestled snugly along the waterfront, many of the town's shops and restaurants were built in the 1870s when industry flourished on the river and the railroad delivered hundreds of tourists.

Clayton, NY

Huckleberry Island is a good place to observe nature. Owned by the Huckleberry Indians Inc., a physical fitness club within the New York Athletic Club, it is used only in summertime. The island's largest residence is the cormorant rookery.

Near Gananoque, ON

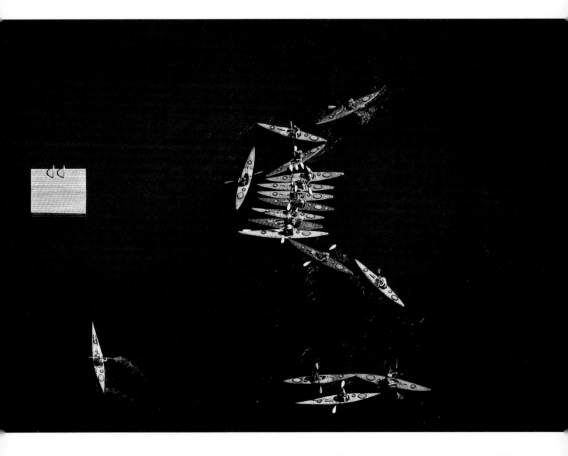

Paddlers flock to a deep-water swimming dock off the sandy shores of Joel Stone Park.

Gananoque, ON

Deer Island was one of the first of the Thousand
Islands to be purchased for a summer escape.
It is owned by alumni of the Skull and Bones
(an undergraduate senior secret society at Yale
University). Famous "Bonesmen" included prominent
citizens such as Buckley, Heinz, and Rockefeller, and
some U.S. presidents.

Once owned by Nathan Straus of Macy's
department store, the grand estate of Belora
and Olympia cottages on Cherry Island was
sold in 1937 to a collector of rare decanters.

Sunken Rock Lighthouse, now solar-powered, was built in 1847 on Bush Island to illuminate the narrow shipping passage between Alexandria Bay and Heart Island. In an 1838 report, Lieutenant Charles T. Platt of the U.S. Navy recommended its construction to increase commerce.

Alexandria Bay, NY

The Thousand Islands archipelago, actually comprising 1864 islands, dots the Canada-U.S. borders along the St. Lawrence River. Fishdam, Bonnie View, and Madawaska Islands are just upriver from the Thousand Islands Bridge.

Near Ivy Lea, ON

Rock Island Lighthouse State Park is located directly across the Seaway channel from the historical community of Thousand Island Park. Listed on the National Register of Historic Places, the four-acre park is accessible only by water.

Fishers Landing, NY

PREVIOUS: Sheets of ice tame the St. Lawrence River in a flash freeze, reminding us that nature rules.

Casa Blanca remains a prominent fixture on "Millionaire's Row." In the 1870s, James Pullman (of the Pullman railroad car) paid $40 for Cherry Island and its original residence, known at the time as Melrose Lodge.

In 1962, Albert and Edith Amsterdam purchased and refurbished the property in Gilded Age style. On public tours of "Grand Dame Edith," visitors can enjoy the romance of days gone by.

Alexandria Bay, NY

The winter deep-freeze seals Sister Island Lighthouse in place. Three islets connected by breakwalls and walkways comprise the Sister Islands, situated just south of the international boundary.

The light, requested in 1859 to mark the narrow course between Grenadier Island and a chain of smaller islands, was not built until 1870. A buoy replaced the light in 1959 and the property is now privately owned.

Alexandria Bay, NY

A snowy road cuts a stark path through hibernating fields. Spring and summer will bring fresh produce from many family farms to local markets.

Gananoque, ON

From the mainland to Howe Island, the *Frontenac-Howe Islander* ferries passengers and their cars year round, 24 hours a day.

The vessel's operating history dates back to 1898. It is now owned by the Ontario Ministry of Transportation and operated by the County of Frontenac.

Kingston, ON

PREVIOUS: Beautiful lines on sleek runabouts hold perennial allure for many Thousand Islanders, who love to zoom along the St. Lawrence River.

Near Kingston, ON

The Sizeland family purchased Hub Island in the 1950s as a getaway, although the unique perch has become a popular cruise attraction. Dubbed "Just Room Enough Island," it contains a small yard from which to enjoy the river view and relax after a quick dip.

Alexandria Bay, NY

A thrilling diving destination, the area is acclaimed for its water clarity, marine life, and seascapes. Explorers can discover shipwrecks from as far back as 1812 lost on the historic Thousand Islands trade route.

A long tradition of fishing is a trademark of the St. Lawrence River. Bass, northern pike, walleye, and muskie entice novice and expert fishers with the promise of trophy-sized catches and serious bragging rights.

FACING: Islands shield the entrance to Smuggler's Cove – a quiet, sheltered area used for protection during the War of 1812. The secluded bay was also popular for hiding boats and booze during Prohibition.

Gananoque, ON

Two princesses admire the fairytale Boldt Castle, which is surrounded by six impressive structures on five acres. With six stories and 120 rooms, it offers much fodder for fantasy.

Alexandria Bay, NY

Singer Castle, one of the last to be built in the area, dominates Dark Island. Initially named "The Towers", it was erected at the turn of the twentieth century for Frederick Gilbert Bourne, producer of the Singer Sewing Machine. The dwelling, which has changed hands several times, was acquired in 2001 and restored by Dark Island Tours Inc. In 2003, the doors opened to the public for the first time.

Hammond, NY

A quick elevator ride to the observation·decks on the 1000 Islands Tower sends visitors up 400 ft. (130 m) to observe the panorama from on high.

Lansdowne, ON

PREVIOUS: Time flies in Frink Park where cruise ships work the waters, and farmers' markets and concerts entertain the whole family.

Clayton, NY

Tiny Bush Island supports Sunken Rock Lighthouse and a boathouse that holds only a slim emergency bunk for the former keeper, who normally rowed from his home in Alexandria Bay to keep the light in good operation.

Alexandria Bay, NY

A vintage boat docks at the popular Antique
Boat Museum, home to the largest collection
of antique and classic boats in North America.
Clayton, NY

PREVIOUS: The Power House and Clock Tower at Boldt
Castle cast a long shadow as a short winter day
ends. The roof was destroyed in 1939 when a stray
spark during a fireworks display caused a fire. After a
complete restoration by the Thousand Islands Bridge
Authority, it opened to the public in 1991.
Alexandria Bay, NY

Powder Horn Island was renamed Calumet Island when New York tobacco tycoon and hotelier Charles G. Emery purchased it in 1882. *Calumet*, the French Colonial word for the Native American ceremonial pipe, refers to this private island's shape.

Clayton, NY

Many of life's simple pleasures can be found at Joel Stone Beach. The splash pad and deep-water swimming dock are great places to kick up your heels with friends.

Gananoque, ON

For centuries, the St. Lawrence River has been a major thoroughfare for vessels travelling between the Atlantic Ocean and the Great Lakes. On the stretch from Montreal to Lake Ontario, ships and cargo from roughly 50 nations utilize the seven locks that operate on gravity, each filling with approximately 24 million gallons of water (91 million liters) in just seven to 10 minutes.

PREVIOUS: A short boat ride from Heart Island brings visitors to Boldt Castle's impressive Yacht House. The worthwhile visit includes a tour of the *Kestral,* an historic 1892 steam yacht, a collection of antique wooden boats (courtesy of the Antique Boat Museum), and some of the Boldt fleet. Also included is a tour of the original crew quarters and the shop where racing launches were built.

Alexandria Bay, NY

Admiralty Islands explorers can rent boats and make their way around places like Halfmoon Bay, Wanderer's Channel, and Mermaid Island. The islands were named around 1815 by Captain William FitzWilliam Owen in an attempt to bring order to area records.

Near Gananoque, ON

Thick marshland outlines the rich natural habitat in Halsteads Bay. River marshes are exceptional places for spotting wildlife such as marsh birds, beaver, and muskrat.

Near Ivy Lea, ON

PREVIOUS: Trees queue along tranquil wintry fairways at Smuggler's Glen Golf Course. More than 300 acres of Canadian Shield, forests, and hills make this an exciting spot to test your skills.

Gananoque, ON

Constructed originally in 1848 on top of a brick house, the Rock Island Lighthouse lantern was difficult to see past the roofline and trees. It was subsequently raised and in 1903 incorporated into a tower on a 30-ft. (9-m) stone pier off the north shore. This improved visibility for ships as they entered the American Narrows.

Fishers Landing, NY

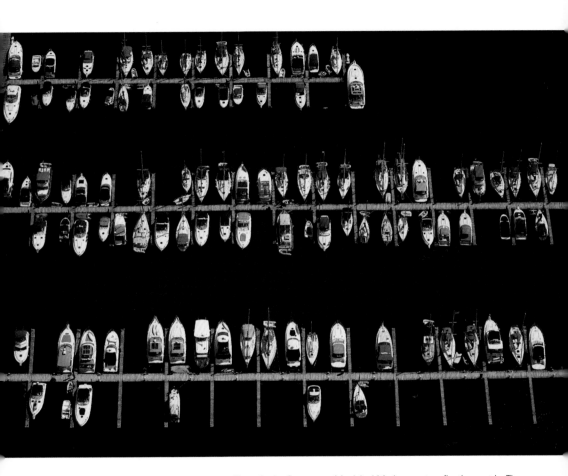

Boats in the Gananoque Municipal Marina create a floating matrix. The
popular 385-slip shelter offers sailors various services.

Gananoque, ON

MICRO MEGAS

A wooden fishing vessel anchors in a town with a proud history marked by traces of the Iroquois and Onondaga. Its European seafaring roots date back to 1615 and Samuel de Champlain. It also provided refuge to Napoleon in 1818.

Cape Vincent, NY

The St. Lawrence River travels 775 mi. (1247 km) from the northeast corner of Lake Ontario to the Atlantic Ocean. The seaway and Welland Canal locks systems lift massive vessels 590 ft. (180 m) above sea level — the equivalent of a 60-story building.

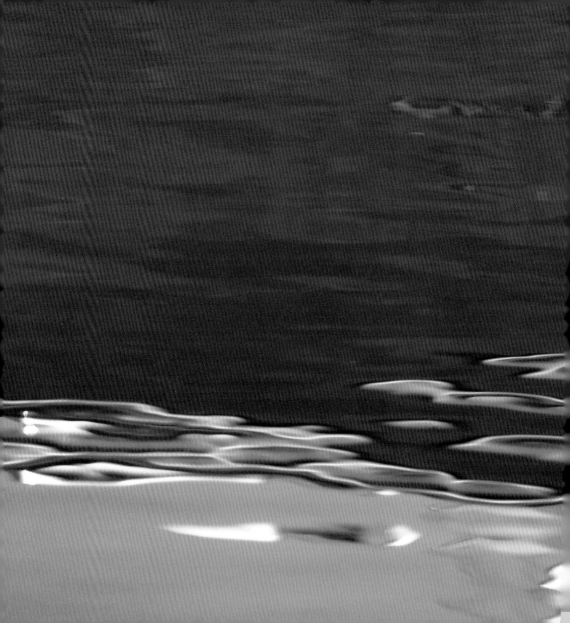

PREVIOUS: Calm blue water reflects the passionate hues of an antique boat, representing an intriguing past of maritime romance.

The Rock Island Lighthouse fades with the dying sun. The 50-ft. (15-m) tall lighthouse was retired in 1955 after a 100-year career.

Fishers Landing, NY

The Stroh family donated the *Zipper* to the Antique Boat Museum in 1975 on the condition that visitors would be allowed to experience the thrill of riding the waves. The museum agreed and now the 1930s-era commuter vessel is a floating ambassador of the era.

Clayton, NY

PREVIOUS: Ripples barely disturb the St. Lawrence River off the shore of Keewaydin State Park. The area is great for camping, fishing, boat-watching, or relaxing in the glow of a warm sunset.

Alexandria Bay, NY

An iconic St. Lawrence River Skiff bobs on the water at the Antique Boat Museum. In 1872, U.S. President Ulysses S. Grant and entrepreneur George Pullman fished the Thousand Islands in Pullman's skiff.

Clayton, NY

An imposing structure, Singer Castle was built by Italian stonecutters using granite from nearby Oak Island. True to medieval and gothic styles, secret passages wind behind the beautiful marble details and walnut paneling, while spy holes allowed residents to peep at guests.

Hammond, NY

PREVIOUS: Helicopter tours offer visitors from around the world amazing perspectives on the picturesque scenery. Unique angles of the world below ensure an unforgettable adventure.
Gananoque, ON

Leisure boats are plentiful and traffic is brisk as the seaway welcomes more than 2000 vessels per season. In the locks, large cargo ships often get the right of way over smaller pleasure craft. Route maps of the Thousand Islands are recommended in trip planning, since the Water Trail clearly marks the recreational channel with red and green buoys.

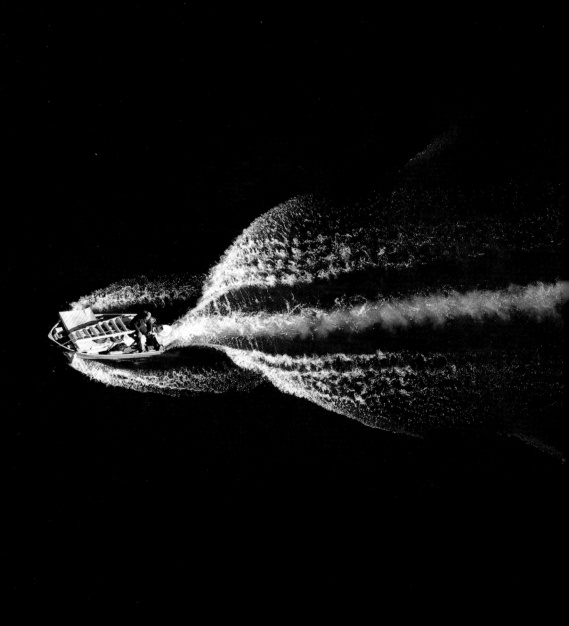

Boldt Castle basks in warm autumn colors on Heart Island. It is owned by the Thousand Islands Bridge Authority, which acquired it for one dollar in 1977 with the agreement that any revenue from tourism be put toward restoration and preservation. Millions have been invested, and the work continues.

Alexandria Bay, NY

The story of Boldt Castle

A stunning tribute to the love
story of famed Gilded Age hotelier,
George Charles Boldt...

Boldt lived one of America's greatest rags-to-riches stories. He was only 13 when he emigrated to America from the small Prussian island of Rügen and started his career by working in hotel kitchens throughout New York City. A few years later, he met and married Louise Kehrer. He soon became the millionaire proprietor of New York City's Waldorf Astoria and the Bellevue-Stratford Hotel in Philadelphia. Together, he and his wife revolutionized the hotel industry.

In the 1890s, the Boldts began vacationing in the Thousand Islands region of Upstate New York. It was there that Boldt purchased the now famous Heart Island, a property he planned to transform into the ultimate gift of love

for his cherished wife. In 1900, he hired a skilled crew of stonemasons, craftsmen and architects to create his own version of a Rhineland Castle.

Work was well underway, with more than $2.5 million invested, when tragedy struck. In January of 1904, Louise died. Boldt commanded that all work on the castle

cease immediately. He never returned to Heart Island.

For the next 73 years Boldt Castle deteriorated rapidly due

primarily to extreme exposure to wind, rain, ice, snow, and vandals. In 1977 the Thousand Islands Bridge Authority (TIBA) was gifted these historic properties and began

its long-term commitment to ongoing refurbishments, securing Boldt Castle's future.

Over the years, TIBA has accomplished the remarkable feat of transforming Boldt Castle into one of the premier attractions in the Thousand Islands International Region. Heart Island's beautiful five acres are a perfect venue for many

weddings, offering enjoyable new experiences with every season. Visitors of all ages can take leisurely self-guided tours of the historic properties using either an audio guide or comprehensive map.

Estrellita (Little Star in Spanish), a small island off the foot of Fairyland Island, boasts a magnificent summer home. Estrellita was built by Andrew Schuler, creator of Schuler's Potato Chips and known in America as "The Potato Chip King."

Alexandria, NY

The epitome of a Canadian getaway, camping under a thousand stars in the Thousand Islands is an experience to treasure.

PREVIOUS: The early morning tranquility surrounding Rabbit Island makes it a very popular fishing location.
Near Gananoque, ON

In winter, Rock Island Lighthouse becomes fully connected to the island with a naturally formed ice bridge.
Fishers Landing, NY

Isle of Pines boasts a large dwelling built in the 1900s that in 2008 gained television celebrity on the popular show *Ghost Hunters*, which investigates paranormal activity. This episode starred the actor Meat Loaf as an investigator.

Fishers Landing, NY

PREVIOUS: Thirty islands comprise the Brock Islands (west of Brockville). Marine traffic keeps the main channel off the north shore quite busy.

Brockville, ON

Making new friends under the summer sun is an engaging way to spend some time.

Near Brockville, ON

At a height of 14 ft. (5 m), the secluded statue of St. Lawrence overlooks the river that bears his name (bestowed by French explorer Jacques Cartier). The nine-ton statue was carved from Indiana limestone by Belleville sculptor James (Jim) Smith.

Near Ivy Lea, ON

Hitting the money shot at Smuggler's Glen Golf Course is a breeze. The championship 18-hole course was designed by Boyd Barr to work with the natural terrain along the river. In deference to the wetland habitats in the Frontenac Arch Biosphere Reserve, he created the "1000 Island Arch" around the fourth and sixth holes.

Gananoque, ON

NEXT: Tucked away from the river's activity, hard-working boats cool down after a full day.

Cycling through warm summer days and fresh breezes off the St. Lawrence River keeps the spirits high. The scenic Waterfront Trail runs 23 mi. (37 km) between Brockville and Gananoque, parallel to the Thousand Islands Parkway.

The river's moods can create gentle ripples that allow paddlers to meander along, or become rushing currents that hustle boats along in a blur.

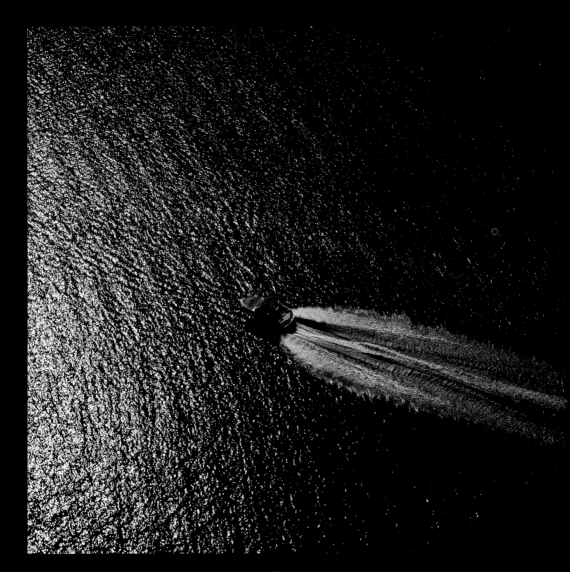

A lake freighter passes Resort Island. Ships traveling in the "Upper Lakes" can be 1000 ft. (305 m) long, although the maximum allowable length for vessels using the Seaway between Montreal and Lake Erie is 740 ft. (230 m) as the locks are only 766 ft. (233 m) long.

Resort Island, ON

A British soldier takes aim in a Fort Wellington military drill reenactment. The fortification originally protected the St. Lawrence River shipping route from attack by the U.S. during the War of 1812 and helped foil the American invasion of Upper and Lower Canada between 1837 and 1838.

Prescott, ON

Kayaking takes enthusiasts close to the amazing wildlife and ecosystem
of the Frontenac Arch – a UNESCO World Biosphere Reserve.

Near Ormiston Island, Gananoque, ON

NEXT: Foreboding clouds in the sky over the Thousand Islands Bridge announce a storm.
Near Lansdowne, ON

The Tall Ships Festival in Brockville livens up the waterfront with colorful sail-pasts, tours, and opportunities to meet the sailors.
Brockville, ON

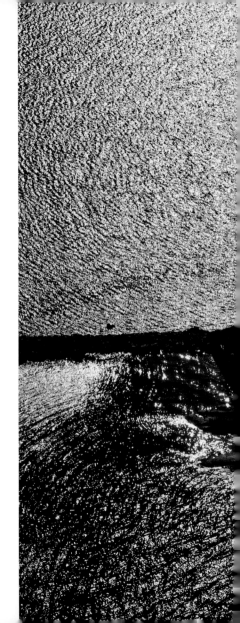

Guests can now dine at Captain Simon Johnston's House (a.k.a. "Kemp House"), which is listed on the National Register of Historic Places. Built between 1880 and 1882, it has been repurposed as a distinctive restaurant.

Clayton, NY

The sumptuous mansions and castles on Millionaire's Row afford visitors rare glimpses into the history, romance, and heartbreak of the Gilded Age.

Designed by Toronto architect John G. Howard, the District of Johnstown Court House and Gaol were erected between 1842 and 1844 by Brockville contractor Benjamin Chaffey. The west wing and Gaoler's House were added later. Once called "Elizabethtown," the city was renamed in 1812 to honor Major General Isaac Brock, war hero and chief administrator of Upper Canada.

Inviting colors encourage friends to stop,
visit, and ponder life along the river.

Frink Park, Clayton

Situated on the bank of the St. Lawrence River and dubbed "the most charming theater in Canada," the Thousand Islands Playhouse comprises two heritage venues.

Gananoque, ON.

Travelers are treated to spirited entertainment as they
board their tour boats for a day around the islands.
Gananoque, ON

Sackets Harbor was a strategic station during the War of 1812, most notably for the construction of naval ships. Today, the Historical Society gazebo overlooking Navy Point Marine and the surrounding park is a peaceful respite.

Sackets Harbor, NY

On Blockhouse Island, a dancing fountain behind
City Hall at the Brockville Municipal Harbor
provides a place to regroup.

Brockville, ON

Fulford Place, an Edwardian mansion, is framed by
an Italianate garden. Now a museum, it is the former
home of George Taylor Fulford who made a fortune
from his patent *Pink Pills for Pale People* in the late
nineteenth to early twentieth century. The medicine
was essentially iron and magnesium sulfate.

Brockville, ON

Frozen on the river, a tiny house battles the whipping winds. The St. Lawrence normally experiences a freeze-up from December to March.

Chasing a freighter downriver at high speed in a classic runabout is a thrilling experience.

Illuminated by the full moon, Heart Island is preserved in ice until May when tourism activity resumes.
Alexandria Bay, NY

NEXT: A fiery-red sunset lights up the window of a small cottage.
Divers enjoy exploring the surrounding waters for the wreck of the
General Hancock, once a car ferry for Governors Island.

Near Mandolin Island, NY

The Ogdensburg-Prescott International Bridge is virtually obscured by fog. The suspension bridge is also known as the St. Lawrence Bridge or the Seaway Skyway and connects Ogdensburg in the U.S. to Johnstown in Canada.

Johnstown, ON

Morning mist rolls in on the river's cool surface.

George Fischer is one of Canada's most renowned and prolific landscape photographers. He has produced over 50 books and art posters along with numerous prints. His work has appeared on the covers of countless international magazines and newspapers, and in the promotional publications of tourism agencies around the world. Two of his recent publications, *Canada in Colour/en couleurs* and *Exotic Places & Faces*, are stunning compilations of his extensive travels. George's book titled *Unforgettable Canada* was on *The Globe and Mail*'s bestseller list for eight weeks and sold more than 50,000 copies. Other titles in the Unforgettable series include: *Unforgettable Tuscany & Florence, Unforgettable Paris Inoubliable, Unforgettable Atlantic Canada, The Thousand Islands – Unforgettable*, and *Les Îles de la Madeleine Inoubliables*. Currently George is working on several new books including *Ontario, Abstract Impressions* and the *Faroe Islands*. His home is in Toronto, Canada.

See more of George Fischer's work at georgefischerphotography.com

ACKNOWLEDGMENTS

My sincere gratitude to those who showed me the Thousand Islands Region and connected me with some unusual adventures off the beaten path: Kathrine Christensen from Tourism 1000 Islands ~ Gananoque; Gary DeYoung and Corey Fram from the Thousand Islands International Tourism Council; Ron Thomson from Uncle Sam Boat Tours; and Ken Saumure for his awesome flying skills. Thanks to Shane Sanford for granting me special access to the wonderful Boldt Castle, and for his interesting historical piece on pages 107 to 110.

Thanks as always to Catharine Barker, the creative director who stages my work in brilliant context, and to editor E. Lisa Moses who is an artist with words. To Jean Lepage who accompanies me and assists with logistics, my continuing appreciation for his invaluable help and longstanding friendship.

Copyright © Miko Barbara Gravlin, artist

152

Antique
BOATS ASLEEP
PLEASE
DON'T "WAKE" THEM

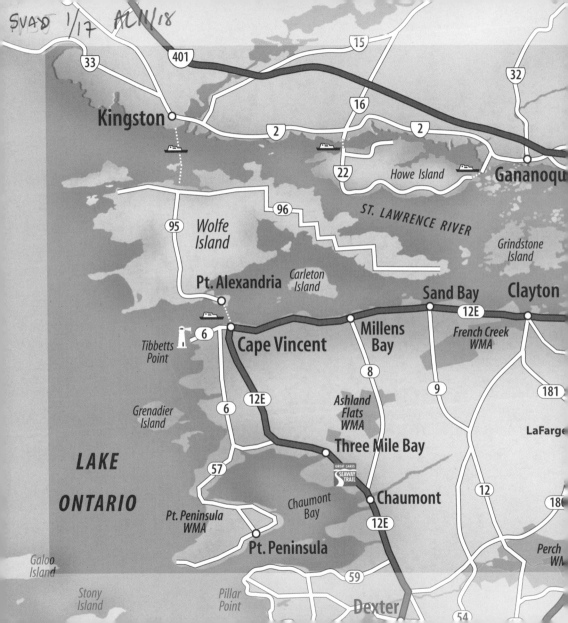